JUL 1 0 2015

D1413568

What is a Nation?

Written by Ellen Kavanagh

Rourke
Educational Media

rourkeeducationalmedia.com

www.rourkeeducationalmedia.com

PHOTO CREDITS: Cover & title page; © Diana Walters, © dustin steller, © Dwight Nadig, © Gary Blakeley, © liangpv, © spxChrome: © Illustrious; page 5: © Victor Soares, © Sadık Güleç, wikipedia; page 6: wikipedia; page 7: © Olga Bogatyrenko; page 17: © Natasa Tatarin; page 9: © Maxim Kulemza; page 12: © Bcbounders; page 13: © Teka Cochonneau; page 12: © jorisvo; page 13: © Lee Snider; page 16: © Dm7en; page 17: © David Snyder, © wikipedia; page 19: © Indos82; page 20: © paulprescott72, © Sindorei, © Phototreat; page 21

Edited by: Jill Sherman

Cover: Tara Raymo

Interior design by: Pam McCollum

Library of Congress PCN Data

What is a Nation? / Ellen Kavanagh
(Little World Social Studies)
ISBN 978-1-62169-913-2 (hard cover)(alk. paper)
ISBN 978-1-62169-808-1 (soft cover)
ISBN 978-1-62717-018-5 (e-Book)
Library of Congress Control Number: 2013937307

Also Available as:

Rourke Educational Media
Printed in the United States of America,
North Mankato, Minnesota

Rourke
Educational Media

rourkeeducationalmedia.com

customerservice@rourkeeducationalmedia.com • PO Box 643328 Vero Beach, Florida 32964

Table of Contents

A Nation

What is a **nation**? Let's find out!

A nation is a group of people who **share** a language, religion, culture, history, territory, or economics.

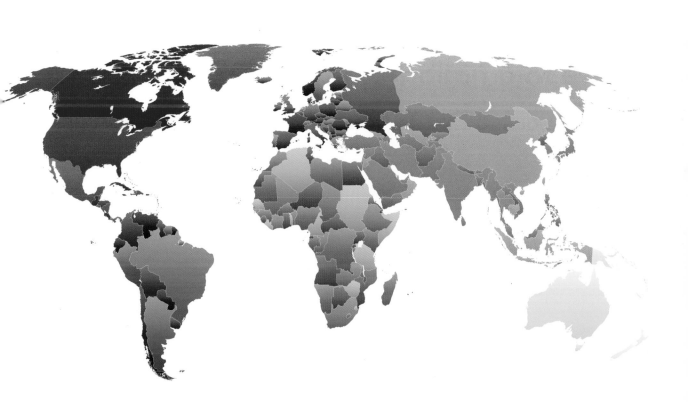

Shared History

Most nations are also **countries**. All countries have physical **borders** and their own government. But there is more to a nation than that.

Common Threads

Here are other ways to think about nations.

Some nations are defined by a shared territory.

The 53 African Nations share a common territory as a uniting feature.

Some nations are defined by a shared religion.

The Vatican is a nation unified by religious beliefs.

Some nations are defined by a shared language.

Everyone who lives in the nation of Japan speaks the Japanese language.

Some nations are defined by a shared economic structure.

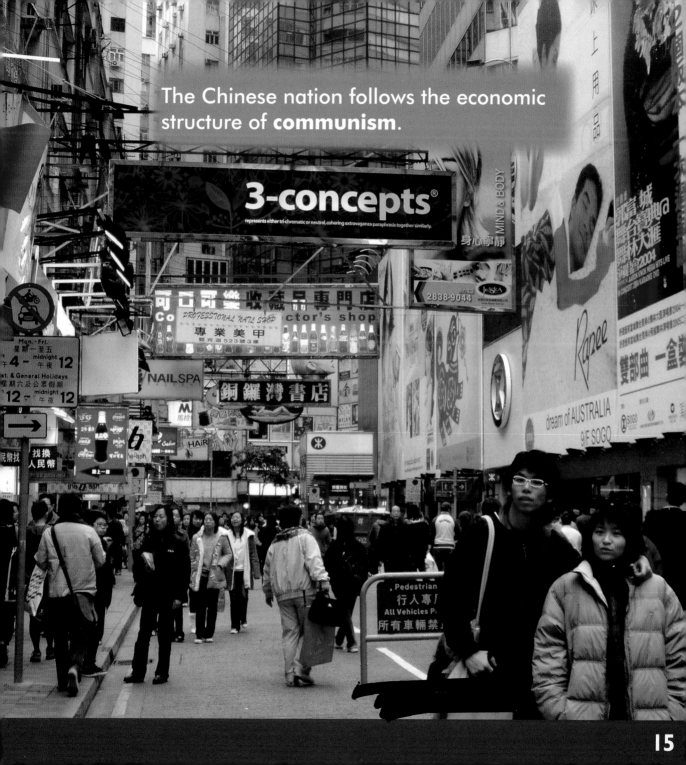

The Chinese nation follows the economic structure of **communism**.

Shared Culture

Not all nations are countries. There are many different Native American nations within the United States. The Native American nations **share** ethnic and cultural customs.

The Cherokee Nation is a group of proud Native Americans who have reshaped themselves to survive and excel as a nation in the United States.

The United Nations

Nations often work together to improve the world. The **United Nations**, an international organization, was founded in 1954. Its goal is to develop relations among nations and maintain world peace.

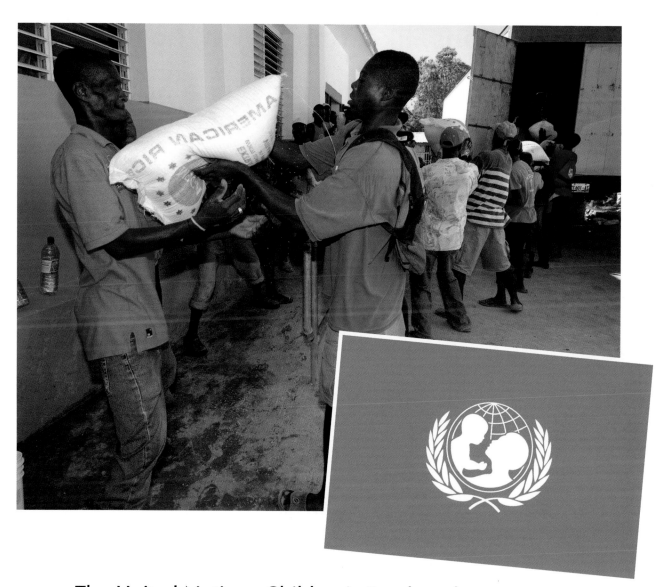

The United Nations Children's Fund works to supply nations in need with food, water, and medical supplies to reduce poverty and diseases.

Some nations, like Yugoslavia, have disappeared. New nations, like South Sudan, have appeared.

After wars in the 1990s, Yugoslavia split into eight new nations including Croatia and Slovenia.

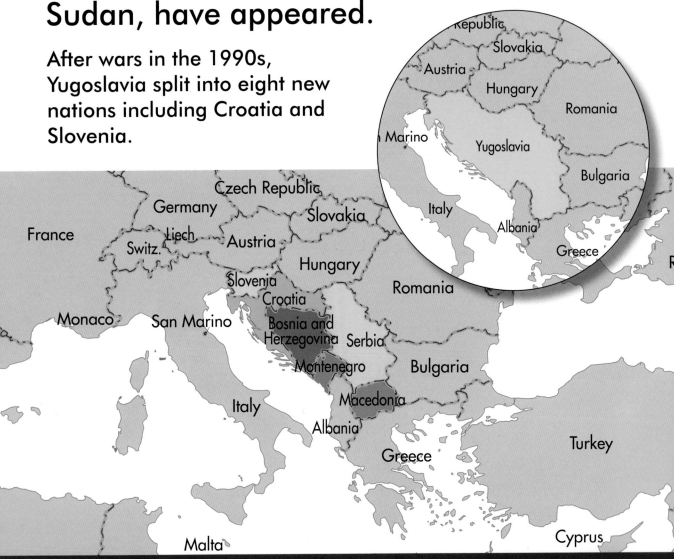

But most nations will continue to be a part of our world.

Picture Glossary

 **borders** (BOR-durz): The dividing line between one country or region and another.

 **communism** (KOM-yuh-niz-uhm): A way of organizing a country so that all the land, houses, and factories belong to the government or community, and the profits are shared by all.

 **countries** (KUHN-treez): A country is a part of the world with its own borders and government.

 **nation** (NAY-shuhn): A large group of people who live in the same part of the world and often share the same language, customs, and government.

 **share** (SHAIR): To use together. To take part.

 **United Nations** (yoo-NITE-id NAY-shuhns): The countries that have joined together for peacekeeping.

Index

Websites

geography.about.com

kids.usa.gov/social-studies/index.shtml

www.socialstudiesforkids.com

About the Author

Ellen Kavanagh has been teaching four and five year olds since 1995. She and her family love reading all sorts of books!

Meet The Author!
www.meetREMauthors.com